THE GEOGRAPHY OF HOPE: POETS OF COLORADO'S WESTERN SLOPE

THE GEOGRAPHY OF HOPE: POETS OF COLORADO'S WESTERN SLOPE

Second Edition

Edited by
David J. Rothman

CONUNDRUM

PRESS

Conundrum Press, Crested Butte, Colorado 81224
Copyright © 1998, 2000 by Conundrum Press

05 04 03 02 01 00   5 4 3 2 1

Library of Congress Catalog Number 00-100892

ISBN 0-9657159-7-3

Acknowledgments

Some of the poems in this manuscript have appeared in the following journals, to whose editors grateful acknowledgement is made:

Bruce Berger:
> *ISLE*: "Haunts of the Mirage," "The Plagiarist"
> *Lightyear*: "Ballad of the Bright Angel"
> *Poetry*: "Ambition," "The Misconstrued,"
>   "Transmigration," "Stout Brahms"
> *Roaring Fork Valley Magazine*: "Trophy Homes"

Joe Lothamer:
> *Chameleon Soup* (Commotion, 1993): "Be a Painter,"
>   "Allen," "October Falls in Black and White"

John Nelson:
> *My Participle's Danglin'* (Majestic West, 1997):
>   "Just Word Wranglin'," "Never Eat Oranges!,"
>   "If a Fish Fell in a Forest," "For Whom the
>   Bells Toll...and Toll...and Toll," "Teed Off,"
>   "If You Knew September"

David J. Rothman:
> *The Christian Science Monitor*: "The Shape of Water
>   Most Like Love"
> *Poetry*: "One of the Lords of Life"

James Tipton:
> *American Literary Review*: "I Want to Speak with
>   the Blood that Lies Down," "There Are
>   Rivers of Oranges"
> *Bleeding Hearts*: "I Wanted You in the Kitchen
>   of My Heart"

CONTENTS

PREFACE TO THE
SECOND EDITION

The first edition of *The Geography of Hope* appeared only two years ago, in the summer of 1998, yet that seems like the distant past in the evolution of Conundrum Press. The original premise was to bring together some of the stronger poets in our region, those who deserve greater recognition within it and beyond it, and then encourage them to work with us to promote the book. The project was successful not only because of the quality of the poetry and the poets' commitment to giving readings, but also, and most importantly, because there is a growing audience eager to encounter poetry about, for, and from this part of the world. We struck a nerve.

I believe that in this book an audience discovered poetry which goes far beyond the local. In their variety, exuberance, and carefully honed craft, the poets in this book—like all strong poets—speak to and for the larger world. As a result, although Conundrum and *The Geography of Hope* began with no distributors, no advertising, and no audience, we are now in hundreds of bookstores throughout the region and beyond, and our original run of 1,500 copies sold out this summer. Jim Tipton, who appears in this book, won the 1999 Colorado Book Award in the poetry category for *Letters from a Stranger*, also published by Conundrum, and many of the other poets have also begun to attract larger and larger audiences.

Given the quality of the work in this book, the commitment of the poets, and the growing audience, I am confident that this new edition will find new readers. There is also a second volume in preparation, which will include new work from the poets in this volume, along with work from some of the other fine poets now working in this corner of the world.

The second edition is largely unchanged from the

first, but is a more attractive book. I have taken the opportunity of reprinting to correct typos, fix margins, and generally bring everything into alignment with the design of our current books. I hope the care the poets have taken with their work is evident; I hope the quality of the edition does them the justice they deserve; and as a result, I hope *The Geography of Hope* provokes you to thought, brings you the kind of news that gives meaning to life, and provides you with some pleasure and solace, which is to say that I hope it does what the best poetry has always done, and must continue to do if it is to be a living art.

David J. Rothman
Crested Butte, Colorado / July 17, 2000

INTRODUCTION

*W*here the Bluebird Sings to the Lemonade Springs (1992), a collection of essays, is the last book Wallace Stegner published in a long and productive life of thinking and writing about the West. In the Introduction to the book, Stegner writes that "the West at large is hope's native home, the youngest and freshest of America's regions, magnificently endowed and with the chance to become something unprecedented and unmatched in the world." These are inspiring and hopeful words for a man in his 80s, and in darker moods in the same book, when contemplating, for example, the desperate foolishness of water policy west of the hundredth meridian, Stegner repudiates them, saying of the West that "neither nostalgia nor boosterism can any longer make a case for it as the geography of hope." The phrase "the geography of hope" is also Stegner's coinage, and when he says he can no longer make a case for the American West as its native home, he is arguing with himself, against himself, over the crucial tensions out of which he made his life's work. In the end, however, despite considerable pessimism about our historical, cultural, and political blunders, Stegner did think that people could come to belong to the land where they lived, rather than merely owning it, even a land as harsh as the West. The vitality of his history and criticism, and the force of his fiction and teaching about it, are testimony to an entire life spent in devotion to that idea.

Stegner was born in 1909 to a poor family with little education, a family that drifted through the Canadian and American West, rarely settling, but like so many others, moving on when things went wrong, or the economy took a downturn. Coming of age as a writer in the 1930s, he didn't feel an oppressive burden of the past; rather, he felt a need to create a past that he could use. As he writes in another essay from his final book, "The Law of Nature and the Dream of Man":

I was always hungry...to belong to some socially or intellectually or historically or literarily cohesive group, some tribe, some culture, some recognizable and persistent offshoot of Western civilization. If I revolted, and I had all the appropriate temptations, I had to revolt away from what I was, and that meant *toward* something—tradition, cultural memory, shared experience, order.

This is itself not a new impulse in America—think of Hawthorne in the Custom-House, struggling to find a worthy American subject for his fiction—and Stegner deserves comparable recognition for articulating that impulse against the background of the great American deserts and mountains.

There are some important differences, however, between Hawthorne's and Stegner's situations, which make the latter's that much more interesting. As Stegner understood, the modes of life that could be transplanted from European shores to New England and other relatively fertile parts of the new world broke down in the West because of the relentless fact of aridity. Civilization requires water, and always has to come to terms with how water circulates through a particular environment, in a combination of adaptation and management. The aridity and tremendous natural wealth of the West led to a boom and bust economy based on extraction and harvesting, which in its turn created a migrant society. While Stegner was attracted to the typically American dynamism embodied in endless migration, Walt Whitman's open road, he was also skeptical of it because of what it does to people and the way and places they live:

[T]he rootlessness that expresses energy and a thirst for the new and an aspiration toward freedom and personal fulfillment has just as often been a curse. Migrants deprive themselves of the physical and spiritual bonds that develop within a place and a society.   Our migratoriness has hindered us from becoming a people of communities and traditions, especially in the West...Especially in the West, what we have instead of place is space.   Place is more than half memory, shared memory.   Rarely do Westerners stay long enough at one stop to share much of anything.

Stegner was one of the writers who sought to discover what kind of shared memory could be found or forged in the West, at the same time as its raw, harsh beauty could be preserved.

This project of seeking a community is what gives such focus and force to Stegner's writing. His motivation was not alienation from any social reality, but an attempt to connect with one, to imagine one that had hardly come into existence, to use the power of words to give meaning to places, including the Colorado mountains, which appear frequently throughout his work. That is why his voice sounds so young and vital even in his eighth decade; he is still writing from young country.

Though not a poet, Stegner understood that it is poetry more than any other art form that can achieve this communing in words, that can draw forth otherwise invisible relations. In another essay from *Where the Bluebird Sings to the Lemonade Springs*, "The Sense of Place," Stegner writes that "no place is a place until it has had a poet...No place, not even a wild place, is a place until it has had that human attention that at its highest reach we call poetry." Stegner believed that the human attention which leads to poetry could grow only in communities, places where people live for generations, and it is what he yearned to see develop in the West, at the same time as he saw the problems such communities often bring with them. Quoting Wendell Berry, he points out that "If you don't know where you are, you don't know who you are."

Hence this book. The poets gathered here all live on Colorado's Western Slope. Some of them have lived here for decades, others only for a few years. They hold a wide range of professions, from student, to Professor of English, to beekeeper, to backcountry guide and outfitter, to painter, to Colorado County Commissioner, to arts administrator, and on and on. They come from Aspen, Crested Butte, Gunnison, Telluride, Silt, Grand Junction, Glenwood Springs, Delta, and other communities, mostly towns, as we don't have but one city, and it isn't a big one at that. Some were born in this part of the world; most immigrated. Some write free verse; some write sonnets; some write both. Some write about the Western Slope; some, even though they may have lived here for a long time, write about other places, or write poems that are not necessarily about places. Their work ranges from the gentle, loving humor of Luis Lopez, to the unforgiving fire of John Cope; from the sensuous, precise observations of Bruce Berger, to the expansive proclamations of Art Goodtimes; from the salty realism of John Nelson to the magical metaphors of James Tipton; from description to philosophy; from the personal to the political; from the sweet to the bitter.

Why make such a list? Certainly Stegner, and anyone else who pauses to think about it, wouldn't expect the poetry of a place, the poetry that helps to make it a place, especially an American place, to fit into neat categories. It's a big country out there. The human attention which we need to give to it if we are to play our part in it has to be equally capacious. Stegner pointed out that a place needs a poet, but while certain places have particular poets—New Hampshire has Frost, Carmel has Jeffers, Chicago has Sandburg—they also have many poets, they have poetry. Jeffers may be the greatest poet of California, but no one would argue he was the only one, or the only great one, with Yvor Winters, Kenneth Rexroth, Gary Snyder, Charles Bukowski, Thom Gunn, Czeslaw Milosz, Robert Hass, Dana Gioia, and so many others all writing in that state. New Mexico has also had its share of writers and artists including Lawrence and O'Keefe; Montana and the

4

northwest have theirs; Utah has Ed Abbey, not much of a poet but a highly poetic essayist.

Colorado has been a bit different. Settled later than most of these states, and in many ways one of the harshest because of its immense mountains, has Colorado produced a great poet yet? Certainly the poets gathered at or near the University of Colorado in Boulder, and at Naropa, have done some fine work, but many of them, like Anne Waldman and Allen Ginsberg, have been visitors who became part of the life of the front range cities, but not that of the mountains, certainly not of the Western Slope. Among the front range poets, long-time University of Colorado professor Reg Saner comes as close as any to staking a creative claim in the mountains, with his lush meditations on alpine nature. A typically evocative passage from one of his earlier books, *So This Is the Map* (1981), a volume selected for the National Poetry Series by Derek Walcott, describes the ecstasy of climbing a high peak:

> I rise through the holocaust of an old burn.
>
> As if fire improving its past
> each smatter of aspen leaf draws its pale green trunk
> some 20, 30 feet up—the branches sassy
> with a chitter and fluff of jays. Once, when it was still
> a breathing universe, these aspen limbs trembled
> that their wood had been nailed
> to the death of a god.
> Above, edge and jut. 10-acre pre-Cambrian thrust
> taking wing on warps grotesque and plausible
> those continuous proofs of the insane.

Saner correctly locates this beautiful place on the Western Slope, but in the wrong quadrant, calling the poem "Mountain of the Holy Cross: San Juan Range." Unless I'm mistaken, there's only one Colorado peak with that name, a 14er in the Sawatch. So even Colorado poets who have been trying to give voice to the Western Slope sometimes have had a hard time of it.

On the Western Slope itself, with its valley towns and high alpine villages, most of which began life as mining camps, and many of which are now gone unless they've been resuscitated by tourism, no poet has yet emerged who speaks to the larger world the way a Jeffers did for California. In fact, if there is any canonized poem about a Western Slope mountain, it is probably Jeffers's "Red Mountain," a true San Juan peak, which he wrote in the early 1930s, when he was a regular summer visitor at Mabel Dodge Luhan's home in Taos:

> Beyond the Sierras, and sage-brush Nevada ranges,
>   and vast
> Vulture-utopias of Utah Desert,
> That mountain we admired last year on our summer
>   journey, the same
> Rose-red pyramid glows over Silverton.
> Whoever takes the rock pass from Ouray sees
>   foaming waterfalls
> And trees like green flames, like the rocks flaming
> Green; and above, up the wild gorge, up the wild sky,
> Incredibly blood-color around the snow-spot
> The violent peak. We thought it was too theatrical
>   to last;
> But if we ship to Cape Horn, or were buying
> Camels in Urga, Red Mountain would not turn pale for
>   our absence.
> We like dark skies and lead-color heights,
> But the excellence of things is really unscrupulous,
>   it will dare anything.

Longfellow, who wrote what may be the other great poem about a Colorado mountain, "The Cross of Snow," is describing Saner's misplaced Mount of the Holy Cross. Longfellow of course never even saw the peak (at least Saner climbed it), relying on an illustration to create a powerful symbol by which to remember his second wife:

In the long, sleepless watches of the night,
> A gentle face—the face of one long dead
> Looks at me from the wall, where round its head
> The night-lamp casts a halo of pale light.
Here in this room she died; and soul more white
> Never through martyrdom of fire was led
> To its repose; nor can in books be read
> The legend of a life more benedight.
There is a mountain in the distant West
> That, sun-defying, in its deep ravines
> Displays a cross of snow upon its side.
Such is the cross I wear upon my breast
> These eighteen years, through all the
> > changing scenes
> And seasons, changeless since the day she died.

Longfellow wrote his poem in 1879, though it wasn't published until after his death. Almost 100 years later, Stegner's 1971 Pulitzer Prize-winning novel *Angle of Repose* has a long chapter set in Leadville. In all these well known examples, the writers created a memorable work, but were not writing from places they called home. If we widen the net just a bit, there is one great exception to this: the late, and unfairly maligned John Denver. I can quote "Rocky Mountain High" from memory:

> He was born in the summer of his twenty-seventh year,
> Coming home to a place he'd never been before.
> He left yesterday behind him, you might say he was
> > born again,
> You might say he found the key to every door.

Denver, and in particular this song, had a tremendous impact on the public consciousness of the Colorado Rockies during the last 25 years, presenting the region as a place of untrammeled alpine beauty so powerful that it could change a life. I know these songs meant a great deal to me as a boy growing up in Massachusetts, though I didn't know then that Denver was writing from this particular region, the Western Slope.

Denver is a truly misunderstood artist. He was a powerful folk-song writer because at his best he knew how to set what are basically small sermons to good tunes. The line about "coming home to a place he'd never been before" seems highly perceptive to me, an honest expression of exactly what Stegner is getting at when he talks about a migrant culture in search of a home. Denver is a highly moralistic lyricist, as in this song, where he is quite serious about comparing his discovery of the mountains—Western Slope mountains—to a spiritual rebirth. The metaphor of rebirth acknowledges something unhappy but unspoken before the discovery, which is crucial to the song's power. As in many others of Denver's songs, a brooding sorrow lurks beneath the sweet melodies, which makes the lyrics more compelling than they might at first appear. In this Denver is much like Longfellow, who has also frequently been accused by weak readers of emotional simplicity, as if only difficult sentences can evoke profound feeling.

Aside from Denver, who was gifted, but not exactly a writer of poetry, I can't think of a single major poet of the Western Slope. In light of the growth going on in this part of the world, and the caliber of the work finding its way into the public realm, the time seems ripe to bring together some of the best poetry this side of the Continental Divide. This area, after all, is a different watershed and therefore a different region from the front range, and from the high plains, and it deserves its own voice.

Each of the poets in this book expresses some of this region's qualities simply by virtue of living here, working here, and making art here. They are of course not the only ones writing in this corner of the world, only a few who have gathered by chance and acquaintance; and if this book succeeds, perhaps we can bring out another featuring still more of this region's writers. But the poets in this book do give me a sense that we are, together, engaged in a common if obscure enterprise, which is the difficult, slow, surprising work of naming.

"What's in a name? That which we call a rose / By any other name would smell as sweet," sighs Juliet, but she and Romeo discover the momentous power of the names they have inherited soon enough. Most of the names in the West remain less burdened by history than were Montague and Capulet. As Stegner understood, they remain closer to those given by Adam and Eve, with the terrifying exception of the Native American encounter with the European invaders. This gives many poets the opportunity, and terrifying challenge, of sewing words up with reality in a generative way. The Western Slope is a part of the world, after all, where we can still climb immense peaks that actually have no names. Surely there's something better to say than "Dawn's rosy fingers touched the granite flank of Peak 13,243." Go to it, comrades.

The West is a big place, and this is a rich book. Humor, love, nature, politics, and magic nestle within its lines, along with sadness, anger, regret, and grief. Yet even in confrontations with the darker side of things these poets are still speaking from young country, describing lives which call out for words. Like all poets, they are imagining ways to live, which has to mean living in a given place, and therefore with each other. Further, although what brings them together in this anthology is a regional fact, I think all of them aspire to put the best possible words in the best possible order, connecting this region to far more than itself. Simply by focusing human attention, putting pen to paper, and then sending their verses out into this place and the wider world, they fulfill a small part of Stegner's vision of the West as a geography of hope, coming home to places they've never been before.

David J. Rothman
Crested Butte, Colorado / June 8, 1998

CAROL BELL

Carol Bell is a former pharmaceutical chemist who left Denver and industry to move to the country eleven years ago. She and her husband now live on a hundred-acre ranch south of Silt, Colorado. After nearly twenty-five years of life among crowds and the city's excitement, she is enjoying her return to the land (she grew up in rural Nebraska).

It was amid alfalfa fields and quiet that she made the decision to learn to write, and she now finds herself deep in the process. Her poems have been published in *Hard Row to Hoe* and *Inklings* magazines, as well as several anthologies.

WHERE HOPE LIVES

for Czeslaw Milosz

Hope appears
when the mud beneath us
licks our toes.

We can't own it.
Eventually the sun claims it,
drinks its moisture
making it
something different,
something the wind covets.

But it is real,
isn't it?
When it crawls
between our toes
on rainy Sundays.

It isn't always reliable
like clocks, for instance,
or rain gauges.

Still, it isn't unreliable,
never sullen
with the noon heat
or angry
when the wind rages.

Maybe it lives its own life
somewhere in the reaches of blue,
and breathes with us
when we remember
the sky tangles in mud
as easily as it stretches to another universe.

Lying in Small Pieces

You knew he
was dying. He lied
he wasn't.
So you ignored
his face as it
became white,
his cheeks so
gaunt his ears stuck
out, and the man
you knew retreated
into his stone house.

You were
not there
to hear him, not
there to see his hands
against the sheets, to
hear the nurses
scurrying, the doctors giving
up. Instead, you welcomed
Medusa who
wrapped you
in her hair,
promising laughter.

You had already tasted
death and
despised it. Like
rank coffee or
broccoli,

like stones that
rest for
centuries forgetting
little bits of their
skin fall away over
decades. Such
small pieces.

You lie
when you say you
didn't know
dying
is about
blindness. You
tell yourself you
did it for
him.

BRUCE BERGER

Bruce Berger was born in Evanston, Illinois, in 1938. He attended Yale University and did graduate work in English at Berkeley until, wondering what Crater Lake looked like in the snow, he left academia for good.

Mr. Berger's collection of desert essays, *The Telling Distance: Conversations with the American Desert,* won the 1990 Western States Book Award for Creative Nonfiction. *Almost an Island,* a non-fiction book about Baja, California, was published by University of Arizona Press in September, 1998.

Though more widely known for his prose, Berger's poetry has been admired for years in literary journals and is frequently anthologized. His first collection of poems, *Facing the Music,* was published in 1995.

TRANSMIGRATION

As kerosene climbs through a wick
Or sap through oak by the slow
Fire of evaporation,
So moisture from the saltpan
Has scaled the flesh and feathers
Of this long-fallen crow
And seeded it with crystals.
Alone with its blue shadow
As if on a shield of snow,
Half scavenger with a tough beak,
Now more than a half vessel
That might have served Versailles,
It challenges the sun
With a blistering salt eye,
Easy in the wisdom
That its fellows are nothing at all,
Serene in its lucky fall,
Its dazzling transmigration
From bird to the stabler kingdom
Of the gem and mineral.

THE PLAGIARIST

Uniformed in grey that so ill-suits
The inner fire; issued only poor
White patches, one per wing, to catch midair
The ardor of the world and hold it there
With flourishes of feints and swoops and flits,
The emperor in civvies finally sits
Imperious upon the topmost bough.
Drumming its tail, throbbing the eye and ear,
It pours the cardinal's pierce and pierce and spear,
The wren's consumptive buzz, the warbler's trill,
Pidgin finch, the thrasher's ill-chucked fill,
The starling's strangled carillon, until
The captive listener can also hear
The annotated cats, the neighbor's phone,
Retreating sirens, second gears, the bits
Of Yeats, the Stevens all acclaiming how
The mockingbird makes every strain its own.

HAUNTS OF THE MIRAGE

Mountains that hung midair
In ghost armadas, lakes
That pinched to alkali
Before your feet found shore,
The Joshua's dry reflection—
All the phantasmal tricks
Of air from the parched surface
That rose and cooled so dense
With refraction that the sky
Lay liquid on the ground
To slake the eye's thirst—
Those haunts of the mirage
Are misted with our breath.
Visionary space
Shrinks to proximity;
Mere doublings of light
Scatter in a waste
Of multiplied exhaust.
By failing to exist,
Sorceries are lost
Before they can be missed;
The tantalizing image
Fails like the recent past;
Specters pull up stakes,
Their requiems unsaid.
Once we understood
The depth to which illusion
Turned on clarity,
Light's quicksilver shades
Joined the other gods
And, disillusioned, fled.

BALLAD OF THE BRIGHT ANGEL

'O happy horse, to bear the weight of Antony!'

(A & C, I,v,21)

Jammed into denim, grinning in Polaroid,
Sneakers and tote bags banging, they lurch and sway
Through Paleozoic sandstone, overjoyed
To be out of their vans at last and chafing their way
Down the ages of the Grand Canyon, and every day
Their mounts are cinched with some new cross to carry.
Only guide and steed are hitched to stay.
O happy mule, to bear the weight of Jerry!

Neck-stroking co-eds, machos loudly annoyed
To be stuck near the rear, matrons who must weigh
More than the chuck box, snake phobics even Freud
Would buck from the couch, equestrians hot to display
Inappropriate talents, students of Zane Grey
Who holler *whoa!* and *giyyup!* in accents that vary
From Youngstown to Stockholm to Dallas to Mandalay—
O happy mule, to bear the weight of Jerry!

Kicking their rental beasts along the void,
Pummeling soft ears with a ceaseless bray
Of past excursions, pizza, paranoid
State troopers, *f* stops, prices in Santa Fe
And the world's most adorable grandchildren, are they
En route to Phantom Ranch or Canterbury?
Who cares with apple cores for overpay?
O happy mule, to bear the weight of Jerry!

Envoi

Fred Harvey, it's a tacky crowd today.
O happy hand, to team up with the very
Jewel of your help than runs on hay.
And happy Jewel, to bear the weight of Jerry!

AMBITION

Think of those naturals who started right off
        blowing horn
Like mad, who were born with terrific prose styles,
Who made principled campaigns for public office
Too soon. They cleared the ground so fast you thought
They'd turn you into someone who knew them
        back when,
And just kept shrinking into thin air until
You forgot to watch, then forgot you forgot to watch.
Now they turn up. They look healthy, perhaps
        even trimmer.
They're just as full of subversion, puns, scenarios,
Are teaching, fundraising, doing little theater,
Have creative homes, a family started, a shot
At tenure or first percussion. They don't even
Seem older, just a bit quieter, and it must be only
You who feel let down. Have they consciously dimmed
Their sights? Revised their timing? Or are they
        withholding
Whole seasons when acedia strikes them dumb?
Even creative homes are cored with midnights
Notched on the bedside clock. Perhaps by day
They spin elaborate counsels to steady themselves.
Patience, they say. One must sit out a time
        without breaks.
One has to let go to regenerate. Nothing gained
By forcing a gift till it blocks. Fruition comes
Of its own accord; meanwhile I must lie fallow,
They tell themselves. I am lying fallow.

STOUT BRAHMS

Sniff for madness—you'll find ripped-up quartets,
Conductorships refused, infatuations
Quenched by the faintest rumor of marriage threats—
And that's about all from the Orpheus of Hamburg
Unless you call mad a shambler's daily ruts
From Vienna digs to his table at the Hedgehog
While his mind commuted bridges of star-crossed notes,
Of flawless subliminations, speechless passions
That flared inside and died like stubbed cheroots:
A life so rarified it rages on,
Articulate fire across five continents
Of furious partisans, now the stout flesh is gone.

THE MISCONSTRUED

They're almost gone,
Whose most rebellious, high-flown
Thoughts obeyed punctuation
Beaten into them by the previous generation.
They got through
The Depression and the War (now World War II)
With direct object and subjective complement
Still chalked on their inner firmament,
Only to watch the peace
Uncross all t's
With the billboard-length infraction, the blurb
That decoupled subject and verb,
The boom in non-
Parallel construction, the one-
Sentence paragraph, the layout framed in prose
That became, in Thurber's word, commatose,
Until police action and protective
Incursion were one with the split infinitive,
And gone was syntax you could syncopate
Because it kept a beat,
And longer gone that parsable country
Where wit and the leading narcotic were extra dry.
Coming to focus before
The whole world was, like, turned into metaphor,
They fade, dismissed, embittered, but
With grammar in the gut.

TROPHY HOMES

Stags from the foundry bugle the front door.
Drifts of shingle veined with chromium drainpipe
Part for the heaven-storming atrium where
Bolts from a cirro-stratus chandelier
On a timer stoke the drama of a staircase
That gyres around a ficus someone dusts.
Failing daylight cues the copper coachlights.
Well-sculpted if unlettered gapes the mailbox.
Come Christmas, braced for with a spangled spruce,
The demigods descend, luscious in fur,
Spilling gifts for caterers, the au pair,
The startled mailman. Corks and snowballs soar,
Ski boots splash the pantry, lights are switched
By rosy flesh, garage doors rise and fall,
The structure blazes like a desert casino.
Before the demigods touch back once more
Come summer, mowers call and edgers keen,
Glads already blossoming take root,
Rackets and clubs deplane, skateboards leap,
Security can relax. And here and there,
Whelmed amid the dormered embassies,
The spec palazzi and half-timbered keeps,
Heirs of the mullioned, dark, eleven-room
Pinched originals that set this pace
Way back, finding their robber baronage
Jet-setted, jettisoned and plain displaced
By its own theme, can hear their deadliest
Epithets—*Conspicuous Nonconsumption,*
Insider Trader Vernacular, Geek Revival—
Die among poodled shrubs as if among
Aisles of an unpopular museum,
Its rotely dusted racks of inscribed cups,
Its bodiless pronghorn gazing with glass eyes.

KAREN CHAMBERLAIN

Karen Chamberlain was born and raised in rural Connecticut and moved west to study veterinary medicine at Colorado State University. She received a degree in zoology and philosophy from the University of New Mexico, and later earned an MFA in Creative Writing from Warren Wilson College in North Carolina. She has studied poetry with Louis Simpson, Galway Kinnell, Michael Ryan, Heather McHugh, and Ellen Bryant Voight, among others.

Ms. Chamberlain has worked at several occupations, including medical research technician, advertising copywriter, commercial fisherwoman, horse trainer, and ski instructor. For six years she was senior writer and associate producer for the PBS nature series, *Wild America.* During that time, she also directed the Aspen Writers' Conference and the Aspen Writers' Foundation, developing programs for writers of all ages. For the past ten years, she has been the literary consultant for the Desert Writers' Workshop in Moab, Utah.

Ms. Chamberlain began writing at the age of ten. She has received a 1983 award from the The Nation/Discovery Program, a 1989 Creative Fellowship in Poetry from the Colorado Council for the Arts and Humanities, and a 1993 Utah Exchange Program Award from *Poets & Writers* and the Poetry Society of America. From 1989 to 1994, she lived on a remote ranch in southeast Utah, and she is completing a volume of poetry and a non-fiction book about her desert experience. A novel and a book of fables are also in progress. She organizes writing workshops for adult and younger writers emphasizing harmony between human and natural communities.

Airlift

As a child I learned from the twisted necks
of Marini's marble horses that what the gods
let out of the sky is serious. Later came
Guernica, that barnful of terrified animals
rolling their eyes at unseen bombers.
This morning, the drone of a single engine
coming in low made me think about the fear
that could drive dumb creatures to such
grotesque poses, made me think how
after half a century, it must be built in,
suspended in air, embedded in unborn flesh.

So I counted it a blessing, in this remote place,
to feel unthreatened by the plane's approach,
to consider instead that it might be bringing
unexpected company. I looked up from chopping
ice on the water tanks, noted the nervous ears
of the horses, and with growing eagerness
shaded my eyes to watch as that precise set
of silver wings banked and smoothly circled
the house three times. My friend! I ran
toward the rutted road, hoping you'd land,
even as the wings tipped and your plane
swooped over straight up-canyon, climbing
as it gave birth to a bobbling streak
of red and green that sideslipped the air,
falling, falling, while your plane flew off
into a sky gone suddenly blue and blank...

This far from telephones or electricity,
friends seem sometimes equally near,
equally distant, and in the daily grind
of history come to me as so much grit
on the wind. In such isolation, it's not rare
to feel the slow burn of joy stinging in my face.
What you brought was the added lift
of wonder, the mad urge to see the world
as Montezuma had, the child's wish
to loose balloons, fly kites, pitch apples,
even rocks or bricks, anything to give back
notice. I wanted to run to the rimrock,
to the top of a nearby cliff, and wave,
wave until my arms blurred into wings
and I took off into the blue, defying vertigo,
gravity, eons of aimless evolution.

        But by then I had run out of
breath, and there, dangling dead-center
from the apricot tree in the front yard
was the red cloth bag and its green streamer.
I hooked it down, and in the bright slant
of winter sun, shook out the weighting:
three pennies and a small dark stick
of driftwood. Then pulled out the gift,
the red envelope on which you'd scribbled
"Airmail/Special Delivery." Inside,
the card, a simple Christmas greeting
closed around the photo of a little boy
gazing down at the sleeping infant
he cradles in his arms. Your sons.

Hard, then, not to think of the flesh
without its fears, not to think of the arms
of your three-year-old, arms he hardly
knows he has, but for the brother
he gently holds. For the rest of the day
I went about chores with a quiet smile,
grateful, yes, for the holding pattern
of these years, yet feeling a flare of anger,
an absurd demand that fate itself
learn fairness. Beyond prayer, that one.
But if it's just too arrogant to go on begging
protection from an unprotected sky,
perhaps it's enough to ask that the care
with which we build our lives, with which
we fly in the face of time, not be dislodged
by any larger grief than we can bear.

INDIAN SUMMER

Yellow leaves swirl
under the streetlight
as I come up the walkway
where today I planted bulbs.
Red tulips. In darkness
not yet brittle with frost
again I smell black
turned earth, leathery leaf,
and think of those shapes
waiting, buried
like ivory skulls of dolls,

while a man whose hand
has just touched mine
drives away into the night.
Inside, I switch off the light
and climb the stairs,
asking for spring, red tulips,
asking for snow, a winter
cold enough for sleep.

Riding the Lion, Riding the Lamb

March wind blows the garden gate
slowly open, slowly shut.
Hard snow spins along the sidewalk,
stipples the bark of the elms,
streaks the withered grass.
Mittenless, empty palms
lifted toward the sky, I catch
nothing. But as the wind subsides,
I breathe with the shift
of snowflakes falling so softly
they seem not to fall,
and feel with what strength
the bare branches of the trees
are attached equally
at both ends.

Stepping in the Same River

I wake to strangled voices
in the air. This is the hand
of August, this wedge
of wild geese delivering dawn

arrow by shadowed arrow
to reeds along the river. Mist
rises from the mud. Face cold,
body warm in a clammy sleeping bag,

I listen to the stream and feel
within me its surface leaping
in white waves unruly with joy,
while the gliding belly beneath

is raked by rock, snagged
by sunken log. Barefoot, chilled,
I kneel on stones to wash my face,
and see my image shatter

in a socket of empty sky. I brace
my foot in broken water. I have
been here before. Cold stone
against thigh takes me back

to a January dawn years ago
when I waded into this same eddy
to stop the slow downriver spin
of a shot goose. My shot, my

prize. What rises in the current
now is not regret, not the gut
turned inside out, but gooseflesh—
dry plumules holding heat

to my skin, the ordered poise
of bedded quills. My arms know
that silken rasp of wind against
wingtip, the sudden falter

into icy water. The limp neck
in my hands is my own.

JOHN COPE

Born in 1934, John Cope was raised in the Berkeley hills of California before the dragon seed of suburbia took root. There he was guided into early adulthood by a highly verbal, opinionated engineer father and a socially graceful, verbal mother who, together, sought the good life in California before Californication.

After acquiring the standard education available to English majors in the colleges and universities of the 1950s, Cope began teaching English at Western State College in the fall of 1959. He taught at Western for the entirety of his working life, retiring in the spring of 1996.

Early on in his teaching career Cope became disillusioned with trying to teach classical literature to students brought up with hard-core practical and pecuniary values of the American West. Unlike his colleagues in the English Department, Cope gave up trying to reverse the loathing of literature with which nature and history seemed to have paralyzed the minds of so many students and devoted his career, instead, to teaching the kinds of practical writing that students in non-English disciplines are expected to use on a daily basis.

To fill the void of no longer teaching literature, Cope began to write it. He found that liquor very much to his taste and continues to imbibe, experimenting with open and closed forms and themes arising from his experiences as a father, sailor, teacher, and human being.

WINTER SKY

Once more a winter sky surrounds my sight:
the grays and blues of weathered planks, rare browns
of earth subdued by snow, the olive greens
of roofs and stalks of pines, the barest hints
of abstract spring. The peaks and sky which rise
above the streets and piney hills consume
mauve colors of the earth, kindling white fire
in space too beautiful and cold for life.

Lily and Rose, April and June are names
for wistful Christian girls who spend their lives
too young, too old—denying time, escaping death.
Girl-child, namesake of cold, white sky, I pray
for you. I hope the lovely name that sings
to me of silences as fierce and bright
as suns sinking toward the western dark
portends a life so brave in facing death.

A low dishonest century has spawned
its own demise: The worst have filled themselves
with passionate intensity, decon-
structing their history in dreams so rife
with ideology the sun goes dark.
The god of Genesis devours the earth,
exhorting men to seize and dominate
the land and sea: fishes that swim and fowls
that fly and all the beasts that walk the earth.

Again, again, the twin
orchids of scrotum sack—power and greed—
have drowned civility and innocence
in rivers of testosterone: bantam
cocks strutting the machismo of war;
frenetic fools screaming of pork futures.
A tragic prince who saw the denouement
consuming all in fire at Trinity.

Shiva, bejeweled, the king of death, serene
dancer of destruction, smiling upon
his last ballet, pointing to his lively
left foot, an emblem of release, one arm
holding a ring of fire, another arm
beating a drum, sounding primordial
pulses of creation, treading upon
dwarfs of ignorance and prejudice.

Brave Winter Sky, the gift I offer you
is certainly about the dancing king:
He will resurrect the colors of the earth
in cycles of rebirth as surely as
the winter sky foretells the spring.
I pray for you to know The Lord, Shiva,
as well as Winter Sky, your lovely name.

SUNSET

Slate-gray waves of day
float down into winter trees,
naked shades
moving among shadows of rose and violet,
contending for dominion
of the west.

I am the rose; you are the violet,
the light and the dark.

I give a toast of prime spirits,
the whiskey we drank
when there were chairs and a fire
to comfort our watching,
and we both spoke.

The whiskey helps me keep you
now the Hamadans and Sarouks,
the China, Meissen and silver,
the beds and tables
and brass fire tools you made
have been disbursed
and I have sold your house:
this architecture,
yours in design,
ours in the building,
these gables and beams and stones.

The fire in the west plays tricks,
or maybe I'm just drunk.
The violet and rose change places.
I cannot see which is the light,
which is the dark.
Are you the rose; am I the violet?

43

COPULA

We are becalmed in haze;
the surface of the ocean
reflects the sky
so I cannot see the line
where worlds meet.

I too am calm.
If I were cool,
my body clean or dry,
if I were not driven by lust
and sucking thirst,
I could be at peace.

When I concentrate,
I see a Brahmin world
where I am merged with the sea
and there is no motion or time,
no desire, no separation.
Terns, small fish,
Portuguese Men Of War and I,
floating, suspended,
predicated only in being.

Is this verb of being,
predicate of my dream
preserver or destroyer,
Lord Vishnu, or Shiva,
his nemesis?

DEMENTIA

The studied slouch of nouns,
oblivious to noon heat,
hangs out, cool, in the street.
But these nouns are not aroused
by the dark beauty of adjectives
insinuating and suggesting themselves
as female shapes of possibility.

Young-buck verbs
self confident
and suited up for the big game,
are stricken unawares:
Bones and muscle seize up
in paraplegic parody
of children who play,
men who build,
women who move.

The patience and control of scholars,
conjunctions and prepositions,
who took their pleasure
in explanations and relationships,
have given way to palsy and stutter.

The sunlight of sentences
no longer rises in the East.
Phrases do not shadow or compose;
you doze, unable to slouch,
hang out, arouse, play, build,
move, or explain.
The green eyesight of the cat
has crawled too close
to your mind's poor birds.

SOLSTICE FOR JOHN

—A simple child,
That lightly draws its breath
And feels its life in every limb,
What should it know of death!—

1.

I cannot see or touch the greening god
who sucks my red blood
and turns my being to wax.
As if a university of pedants
had composed the last act,
conjunctions tangle like propylene rope,
yanking my life away,
hobbling my spirited sun
in his northward passage
through the celestial sphere,
my torrid zone.

The night is good, no doubt,
and I must learn by going
where I have to go.
Yet the evening is bright
and I shall rage against the night,
blow storms from the North Atlantic
through a winter of discontent:

2.

Wordsworth seized upon a faith
that looks through death.
It spawned the "philosophic mind,"
serial killer of his poems,
pretending to console him
for murdering the child within.

In April, for the hundredth time,
I met that faith face to face.
Mouthing cliches, a ritual of death,
it spluttered
into the grave of a friend,
like spit.

Cassocked, bearded, looking human,
imploring, demanding approval,
it faded in my mind
as grotesque music died,
at last, more silent than the corpse,
my friend.

3.

As Christians, I know Nature
for a brute that eats and shits
itself to death.

In a mania of madness,
a lust to transcend the alimentary,
my father destroyed himself
with dreams he could not achieve,
died insane in a nursing home,
managed to serve every alimentary need.

Howard, companion of my youth,
pegged out at forty-eight.
Mary, my mother,
who shared my father's dream,
taught kindness to the air and ground,
gave up her ghost at sixty-three.

I have cancer myself,
am waiting, as I write,
for a technician's phone call—
facts to help me navigate
the flood of time toward death.

There hath passed away a glory from the earth.

4.

A boy in a boat calls to me
from within.
Banging to windward
he swims like a trout,
soars like a hawk,
pulling the tiller to windward—
merging past, present and future,

the sky, the wind, the lake,
the small sloop, himself,
joining all in the palm of his hand.

Heedless of tangled plans,
the politics of defeat,
I parent that boy,
teach him to sail.
I love him more than my life,
because he knows the immortal lake
as spray upon his skin,
wind in his face,
the tiller's pressure upon his hand.

5.

Once there was joy in ideas.
The rush of reaches in heavy air,
through seas of thought,
writing all day,
finishing with beer among friends,
understanding without speaking.
Thought resolved in silence,
as in poems.

Now there is incessant talk,
intelligent qualification,
acceptance of death,
cutting losses,
managing failure,
suffering fools,
tracing the tangles
of rope.

The old power of reaching,
rushing through the calm of being,
is becoming chatter
with colleagues at lunch.

6.

A feeling of reaching, in a calm of going,
sailing the lake of being and thinking,
can be induced with drink.

It fools the boy
within,
sickening him and me,
in a virtual reality game
of death.

In the rush of reaching,
it stimulates
the touch of angels
more tragically
than crucifixion;
betrays the boy
more surely than nature,
pedants or priests.

7.

How shall I navigate this Tropic of Cancer,
guide my boy in a boat,
touching, feeling
pressure aginst his hand,
knowing, reaching, through the calm of going
off the end of the earth?

8.

I am a god of the river,
boy in a boat drifting
feeling, touching, moving
in currents of water and time
through the souls of the dead
into the lives of the living,
flowing, going as love and awe
out of the lake of being
into the unimaginable sea.

ART GOODTIMES

A one-time candidate for ordination in the Popish rites, Goodtimes was born in the postwar boom to a Pacific Rim working class family. He completed formal training in rioting at San Francisco State, with refresher corses in Sixties tribalism at various Rainbow Gatherings. He's taught pre-school, been a construction laborer, shoveled snow off condo roofs, directed a community art council and worked as an editor/journalist. Currently he serves as president of the Telluride Institute and as a San Miguel County Commissioner from the Norwood area—Colorado's highest-ranking Green Party elected official.

Goodtimes has five chapbooks to his name, including *Embrace the Earth* (Homeward Press, Berkeley, 1984), and *Mushroom Cloud Redeye* (Western Eye Press, Telluride, 1990). He's published poems, essays and articles in dozens of newspapers and periodicals around the country, including *The Sun* in North Carolina, *Petrogylph* in Utah, *Wild Earth* in Vermont, *Earth First! Journal* in Oregon, and *High Country News* in Colorado.

In 1989 he received a $4,000 poetry fellowship from the Colorado Council on the Arts and since 1988 has been directing Talking Gourds, an annual Four Corners bardic poetry gathering inspired by his teacher, Dolores LaChapelle. He makes his home at Cloud Acre in the San Miguel Basin of the Colorado Plateau.

ROADKILL COYOTE

sprawls across the centerline
backleg broken * round glazed
eyes glassy as marbles
unwavering * unblinking
as the world rolls by
now unnoticed or maybe
all seen & thus merely
unremarkable * no fudge
or flinch of instinct * just
the cold last look of it all

i turn the car around &
go back to the body * drag her
off the road * steam rises
when i stroke her flanks
the jaw locked open * canine
teeth menacing even in death

i take out my knife * sing
a death song & thanking coyote
i cut off her tail
fur too beautiful to bury
& then pull her hind end
deeper into the rabbitbrush
beside the highway's shoulder

all the way home * down
the canyon & up Norwood Hill
singing her
back into the mystery

JOJOPAN

Walking early morning light.
Bunchgrass tufts still wet with dew.
Mist lurking off the cliffs.
I find shell mounds beside the footpath.

A midden vein of crumbling bone
exposed. Cut into. This is all
that's left of Jojopan.
                        Open wounds
on the south bank bluffs
of the Big Sur River.

Sargenta Ruc
                the Rumsens called it,
lost village of the Esselen.
A people gone like grizzly.

Mysterious ones. Shamans
who carved their secrets into rock
along Church Creek. Who painted red
& black mosaics. Sun discs. Winged gods
who flew across the sandstone.

In a cave near Tassajara
a wall of hands. A cloud of white
prints dancing on stone
hints at some forgotten rite.
Solstice. Moonlight. Initiates
pressing skin against rock
& the rock remembering.

Here above the river beach. Deserted
bluffs. Scavenger gulls wailing in the wind.
I kneel beside whitened clams.
Ash-black soil sprinkled with musselshell.

Upstream past a grove of eucalyptus
I can see the old adobe of the English
sea captain who married his señorita
& homesteaded a Mexican land grant
in the delta terrace of the Rio Grande Sur.
New shingles gleam in the sunlight.
Roof & walls carefully restored:
"an historical site worth saving..."

The land around it also saved. Protected.
Fenced in. The signs say
Molera State Park
named for a wealthy dairy rancher
famous for his parties and jack cheese.

Beyond the adobe
there at the feet of the San Lucias
I can see Hwy. One as it swings east
slicing through the Esselen homeland,
its paved serpentine crowded
with scenic landmarks & historical markers
with parking lots full of sports cars & Coupe de Villes
with private healing spas & off-limits hot springs
with rustic cafes serving Big Sur burgers
with bookstore fishnets sporting their spring catch of pulp
with roadside stands of redwood burl table tops
            going cheap

with acres of Ticketron campsites booked solid
with landscape galleries framing the impossible
with gas stations pumping dinosaur oil
with smokeybear rangers landing in whirlybirds
with retired dentists from Pasadena wheeling by in
    their Winnebagos

& not a thing to tell you that
       effehi
a people lived here
      kiskat na mismap
thousands of years
      pacima kenatsu
weaving nets
    kespam nenipuk
chanting songs
    iyu iyu
dancing
  the language of dreams.

Malitahpa.
 Malitahpa.
  Malitahpa.

There is nothing.
   Nothing.

LEARNING TO SMILE

"I follow Freud's opinion that at birth there is
no consciousness, accordingly, that there can
be no awareness or conscious experience...
Thus it is rare to find the smiling response
before the third month of life."

*The First Year of Life: A Psychoanalytic Study of
Normal and Deviant Development of Object
Relations*

Rene Spitz

Floating in the sac
I sucked the blood of my mother's cigarettes.
Her breath fed me.

When kicking in her belly I began
to make my move, they rushed her
fast car & sirens
to a monolith of brick.
Laid her flat on a gurney
& wheeled her helpless
into the sterile room of deliveries.

We both felt the sudden vertigo
the whirl & loss
as the anesthetic took effect.

Unconscious
drugged into dreams
she was made to push me
out of the house her body had been.

Unconscious
I slid head-first
into the assault of their bright lights
forceps, antiseptics.

A masked man held me captive
upside down.

Too soon his rubber gloves
cut the cord that pumped me
mother's air mixed with blood.

Too soon.
My face turning blue
asphyxiated, brain throbbing
until those brusque hands
hung me by my heels
& slapped the life into me.

Still groggy from the drugs
was it any wonder that I cried out
howling at the world?

Raw atmosphere jammed my lungs
Silver nitrate burnt into my eyes.

I was born craving nicotine
& the smell of her skin,

But they hauled me away
to be tagged, guarded
& quarantined.

My own father, criminal with germs
allowed only a peek through glass
at his first-born son.

There in the nursery
tended by strange, masked women
I was given a blanket to calm my fear.

So my first bond was made
with impersonal cloth.

First comfort found in hugging the material
close around me
as later in times of stress I would grab hold
of objects as though they
could help soothe the loss & aching.

There in the arms of obstetrics
my heart dangling from the thread of
its own frightened beat, I slept
& slept & slept.

My body retreating into shock
that instinctual safety valve
releasing me
from the merciless onslaught of
modern technology.

And then they wondered
why I cried
when they hauled me back
to the birthsmell of the Mother.

Why I couldn't focus
& look her in the eye.

Why it was months
before I learned
to smile.

THE ART OF GETTING LOST

for George Sibley

excuse me, pilgrim
could you tell me
the way to the next wilderness
parking lot?

heh, man—get lost!

but before you lose it
look closely
because
it's not so much you losing it
as the place that takes you away

it's slickrock deer trail thick with juniper
takes you away
it's Mancos shale wild strawberry avalanche chute
takes you away

& suddenly olla kala panta rei
you're just another
neopagan zenmother Buddhada
learning pandemonium
toking pure chaos

cougar in the headlights
takes you away
hairstreak in the rabbitbrush
takes you away

or maybe it's at a table over breakfast
where some resort town waitron
Venus Kali clone
takes you away

& falling in love
you lose it

take Luna in the mushrooms & quackgrass
rolling in it on Sheep Mountain
that first green-eyed summer

or take that infamous hike we took
to the San Miguel Canyon petroglyph
that scribed a hoop in the earth
& led us back to our beginnings

remember
you can't lose
what you haven't found

crouching for shelter from Shandoka's lightning & ice
takes you away
clambering hands & knees up Lone Cone scree
takes you away

getting so lost
you find yourself

Canyonland cliff shelf narrowing to goat hold
takes you away
Uncompahgre's Tabeguache pine scratched by bear
takes you away

one minute next-to-death
& then
born again & again & again

toad kachina grotto vision on Nuvatik-ya-ovi
the San Francisco Peaks
takes you away
Big Sur hot spring crotch-of-the-redwood full moon pool
takes you away
Pacific Rim combers in a Salt Point storm
slamming down fists
takes you away

letting go
enough
not to panic
but to play it like a tune
whistled & hummed
as a hymn to the Mother

easy bro, Haleakala's charm
takes you away
yo, eating mangos & making love
in the sea cave at Kalalau
takes you away

this IS my religion
I believe in being lost

& everything I find on the way
esta milagro
& what finds me
I try to field

adventure not predicament
chasing chaos
just as much as calm

the only straight lines in the headwaters
are the rifle's scope
& the map's compass

so, scram pathfinders surveyors engineers
gimme the loon's zigzag walk

let me lose it
I know how to use it

SARTOR RESARTUS

All we can expect are
pockets though we dream
dress pants,

wild utopian ties
& some secret Cenozoic
sense of balance.

Of place.
Of life re-membered.
But can't you see?

The tailors have gone to sleep
with their TV sets on. Bleep. Bleep.
And the future's job will be mop up

with whatever
buckets, brooms, smuggled
Green baggage or toolbags of deep tricks get left
behind. On purpose or by worldmind's chaotic chance.
Dance. Divine tarantella.
That is
by you & I. The ancestors.
Needles in the weave of
all
creation
yet to come.

L u i s   L o p e z

L uis Lopez teaches in the English Department at Mesa State
College in Grand Junction, Colorado. He has a Ph.D. in
Medieval English Literature from the University of New
Mexico, and an M.A. in Liberal Arts from St. John's College in
Santa Fe. He has had poetry published in anthologies and
literary magazines, including *The Americas Review, Fan,
Piñon, From the Heart,* and two poems published in the 1997
Spring issue of *Karamu,* devoted to humorous subjects. In
April, 2000, he published two volumes of poetry: *Musings of
a Barrio Sack Boy* and *A Painting of Sand.*

He is also a playwright. One play, *Dia de Visaticiones,*
has been produced on stage in both Albuquerque and San
Antonio. He has also written *Gina* and a one-scene play titled
I Don't Know Nothing.

Luis is a native of Albuquerque, New Mexico. In addition
to his duties at Mesa State College, Luis teaches Latin at Grand
Junction High School.

ONLY NOW I REALIZE

your Radiola recording of the Amos 'n Andy Show
brought to mind those winter evenings
when Mom and Dad sat on the couch in the dark
and you and I lay beside the coal-burning stove
        the four of us
lost in a succession of half-hour worlds
        each of us
chuckling at Fibber McGee's clattering tumble
at Charlie's maneuvering Bergen
snickering with Baby Snooks
laughing at the Schnozz
at Digger's "I'll be shoveling off"
and patiently accompanying Benny to lock
after rusting lock down basement stairs
to the ancient vault holding his famous hoard
        only now I realize
it is not so much those half-hour worlds
that moved me as the closeness we shared
in the dim light of the Philco dial and the
slow red glow of her Camel and his Chesterfield

NEHI Strawberry Down-and-Away

When the NEHI Strawberry pop bottle cap
curved down and away
just below the blur
of your reaching broomstick bat,
I knew I had you.

"Strike One!"

Eugene yelled from his seat on an orange crate
a few feet behind the plate,

but you stood there unruffled
and dug in for the next pop bottle cap,
your bat swinging back and forth just before
you cocked it, elbows up, behind your right ear.

I bent down and reached
into the bucket of bottle caps beside the mound.

One NEHI Strawberry left,
kept for just the right moment.

So I selected a 7-Up up-and-in
since I knew you were expecting
the RC Cola low-and-just-barely-outside.

You were creeping up on the plate.

I did my Satchel Paige-loose-and-lanky wind-up
and
handcuffed you up-and-in on the wrists.

"Strike Two!"

Eugene yelled, and this time you stood there
dumbfounded,
bat never leaving your shoulder.

Then that Babe Ruth insolence crossed your face,
but I could see worry in your eyes.

Would it be the NEHI Strawberry?

I reached into the bucket
and took the Coca-Cola down-and-in.

If you didn't offer,
I'd come back with the Orange Crush
pull-the-string-and-break-your-silly-back.

You didn't,
so I concentrated on the Orange Crush
with the count at one and two.

Boy, did I pull the string!

But it landed plop at your feet
bringing the count to two and two.

I saw your eyes gleam
with new confidence, and you could
hardly wait for the next pitch.

You stared at me.
I stared at you, but I mouthed
NEHI Strawberry
to shake you up a bit.

I reached out for the NEHI Strawberry,
but my fingers closed on the NEHI Rootbeer.

I knew you'd never forgive me
if I got you with that.

I let it fly, but as I let it go, I realized I didn't
go underhand.

Your wrists snapped.

WHAP!

The cap zipped past my ear,
stinging the air,
then clattering on pavement clear across the street.

A line drive home run!

You danced like an Indian warrior,
whooping and yelling,
beating the plate with the broomstick.

Then you stopped and pointed a haughty finger
out over the center field fence
while I stood there, head down, dejected,
staring at the NEHI Strawberry in the bucket.

TO A COAL MINER IN MADRID, NEW MEXICO

no hoof, no foot, no wheel
lifts black dust
from coal mine floor
to grit and grime and gunk
your lungs

not now

now your effort
to breathe
causes
heavy lids to close
over ever-tired eyes
in hope of precious sleep

but when you sleep
the demon sounds
of cracking rock
and tortured wheels
whirl into twisting storms
that tear back and forth
across the floor
of your fevering brain

uncovering layers of dust
from a body
lying face up,
forcing it to rise,
the mouth to cough
black dust,
the eyes to well tears
that wash down coal-crust
cheeks, white rivers
revealing your own face,
frightened eyes staring
into your own

until the storm ceases,
the body crumples,
the coughed dust settles,
layer upon layer,
a thin black veil,
sorrowful
shroud, over you

"Holy Mary!"
you gasp as you awaken

IMAGES OF SAN LUIS

Often of late
And far from this poor
Tin-roofed-made-to-look-like adobe church

I have seen a votive candle burn low in a red glass

Sole illumination in this dark corner
Of a chipped plaster image
Of San Luis de Gonzaga
Church patron
Standing two feet high
Yellowing surplice over faded black cassock

Eyes downcast, seeking heaven

This is where my father stood to make his peace
When times were difficult to
Ask forgiveness of stubborn sin through his namesake

And where I now stand
Drawn from afar to make my difficult peace
With the memory
Of his tobacco and whiskey breath

ABIQUIU

composed at Ghost Ranch

Take this city-filled
soul,
pour it out,
place it in soil
beneath
your high desert vista.

Fill it with canyon,
sky,
mesa,
mountain,
smell of rain
and
song of bird.

Tint each
with time of day.

Let each
settle
into a painting of sand

so that when I'm away
I can
close my eyes
and gaze upon
and breathe your sacred strands.

TOMÁS

Mamá. Go see for yourself.
Puro had babies. He's under the porch.
Listen. You can hear them from here.
I wonder how many.
I can hardly wait to give them names.

Santa niño, Tomás.
Puro can't have babies. He's a he.
Además, es un perro, and dogs
Can't have kittens. Only las gatas.
Que imaginación tiene este niño.

But Mamá, it's true.

Tomás, if you tell lies,
Your tongue will turn into a snake's,
Como dice en la sagrada biblia
Cuando Adán mordió la manzana en Eden.

Pero Mamá…

And no one will believe you when you
Have to tell the truth.
El niño Jesus never told lies,
And he made his mother very happy.

But Mamá, you can hear them from here,
And, anyway, the priest told a big lie
At church on Sunday. He told the people
That baby Jesus was born of a virgin.
Everybody still believes him.

Ay Tomás. Go name the kittens.

JOE LOTHAMER

Joe Lothamer lives in Gunnison, Colorado where he has been painting and writing poetry for over eighteen years. Since being inspired by the work he did in the early seventies with Greg McBride, a silk screen artist in downtown Denver, he has proceeded to explore expression in paint and words.

Joe has shown and sold his work throughout the country, notably in Colorado, Washington, Wyoming, South Carolina, and California. He has participated locally in the Gunnison Council for the Arts and the Alliance of Visual Arts. He served for three years as Director of the Summer Arts Institute, a program for children. He participates in the spoken word performances, *Wild Word*, produced by the Center for the Arts in Crested Butte, Colorado.

Joe's work is shown at Johnson's Gallery in Gunnison, the Rendezvous Gallery in Crested Butte, and Jacketree in the Lodo area of Denver. His first book of poetry, *Chameleon Soup*, is available through The Book Worm in Gunnison.

He is currently working on a novel.

Be a Painter

write with color
completely with incomplete syllables
words sentences phrases
whole novels in red
use green like a bayonet
yellow vowels
blue consonants
utter vulgar violets
on white comments
forget brown innuendoes
black blocks on lemon triangles
indiscrete testimonials of hues
beyond vision
unseen by the eyes
yet heard by the conscience
muttered with dumb lips
into hollow ears
still heard
wind into water
be a painter
brush tiny details
in masses of angry colors
a general
rallying troops of rebelling sailors
across a desert pink sea
talk of emotions glaring thru
illogical curtains
curtains of gold
the gold of air
not idols or rings

gold of finest silk
in folds upon flesh of pale
ochres and siennas
throws of light
crystal shards that stick in you
way in beyond you
take a look
look at what isn't there
don't explain just look
look
be a painter
a blind man
white cane
tapping a solid illusion
ridiculous tonal variations
incomprehensible
you judge it you rationalize it
forget perspective obliterate it
the view
is behind you
you are being observed
observed and rejected
you
does sense mean something to you?
be a painter
be a painting
not a finished masterpiece
but an ongoing struggle a war
an explosion
be a piece of paint
paint a portrait
paint yourself

be a painter
be a painter
live in a basement
take drugs
paint the same painting
for two years
tones over tones
background over background
put the same color over itself
mix it to match
no one will know
stop taking drugs
stop licking your fingers
have sex with yourself
use yourself as a sense object
you can tell yourself
we can still be friends
get a job a real job
one that pays pretty good
make money
dream about being a painter
quit work
sell to tourists
western scenes
sell black velvet paint by numbers
to corporations
get yourself a prize
sell for thousands
make them beg
live off your wife
do a painting to pay off
your traffic fines

cover up an island with plastic
put a pair of panties across
the great divide.
buy a pair of sunglasses
wear them backwards
cut your ear off
shave your ass
grow a beard
dare to be
the same as everyone
act like a spoiled brat
get humbled go to jail
be a painter
dream of being a janitor
be a painter
be a success
be famous long after you're
gone
people will make you a hero
they will know the opinions you
never had
you will be envied
for money you never made
you will be respected for your work
you will be
long gone
be a painter
be a painter
be
a
painter
be a painter

go to Rome look at the chapel
go to school
let them shape your talent
develop a mental block
live in a trailer
make pictures too big to
get out the door
tell everyone you're ok
tell yourself
you're okay
be a painter
listen intently while people tell you
they know someone who paints
who is really good
and they make lots of money
wake up painting
paint for lunch
eat coffee
don't take yourself serious
don't even spell itt right
become invisible
stop using logic
don't even think about what you are doing
sell tapes of your art
describing what it looks like
write poems about
being a painter
be a painter
be picasso be rembrant be matisse be simbari
or salvador dali be o'keefe
be an unknown be Joe
be a painter

do what you want
but
for your own sake be a painter
yeah a painter
yeah
draw eyes
only eyes without faces
draw on impulse eyes only eyes
romantic eyes lines of eyes
draw eyes on bed sheets
crying eyes laughing eyes moodless eyes
one eye a spirit eye
do this for hours   days   years
use a flair pen on white paper
throw away your eyes
paint
paint
paint
be a painter

ALLEN

You really got thru to me
When I first saw a poster of you
in 67 with your wild guru hair
and that red eyed hippie faggot stare
you busted Mamon
revealing everything denied
by a fifties society
Questioning all that was trusted
"Love, Peace, Pot," says the mystical poet Jew
but don't get caught!
I saw you in a park in Denver I can barely
remember those hazy musicians playing
saying they were the grateful dead
You took the stage as flower children
withered away, sat there crosslegged
and made sounds like a cow...Om, you sighed
as the crowd cried for more rock and roll
you offered no towers of fairy tale to hide in
only portraits of our real selves reflected
in your eyes

October Falls in Black and White

In this country
          of drizzle and frost
Rain born black clouds
          thin as silk paint
ripped from a blue fence in a
          harvested country
Brilliant penetrating
          dense changed
final songs arranged
          on dazed crumbling
          strings
Everything arrayed
          bringing fruit down
Leaves, summer grain
A dance of delicate shimmering legs
A rebirth of astonishing grace
Winds weave over grey gates
Spilling forgotten seeds
in this
ancient sunken place

JOHN NELSON

Since 1978, John Nelson has owned and operated The Gunnison Country Guide Service in Gunnison, Colorado. Besides being a guide and outfitter, John has worked as a ranch hand, range rider, high school teacher and coach, and any other work necessary to survive the long Gunnison winters. John began reciting poetry around the campfire to entertain guests, other wranglers and guides. When one guest remarked, "John, you're good at reciting other people's poetry, but have you ever written any of your own?" he began writing and performing his work around Gunnison, Crested Butte, and other parts of Colorado. Much of John's poetry is based on his experiences in the outfitting business, working with horses and mules, other guides and outfitters, cowboys, and of course, "dudes." He continues to perform many of the works of other contemporary and old-time cowboy poets in addition to his own material.

JUST WORD WRANGLIN'

Sometime a while back it seemed real clear to me,
T'was time to take bein' a cowboy poet seriously.
I'd get some professional advice, do it properly,
From the Department of Language Arts at W.S.C.

Well, a few calls later, I had what they said for sure
Was a high browed expert on verse and literature.
With a "matter of fact" voice, she seemed real sweet.
So, we set a date and time that we both could meet.

Then, I sent her some poems, my very best to date,
Full of cowboy wit and charm that she'd appreciate.
This would give her some days for appraisal time.
And when our date came up, I went to learn
            about rhyme.

Well, it didn't take long before we had to disagree,
When she insisted that my verse ought to be free.
Heck, as long as it took for me to make all this rhyme,
I can't see where it'd hurt to be paid for my time.

Then she pointed out that all my negatives was double,
And I had too many pronouns that could cause trouble.
But it ain't no problem, not nothin' to worry about.
Don't them pros and cons all seem to balance out?

She says, mate plural verbs with single nouns less,
And how it's proper to cut an ear off irregardless.
But, she's got me confused, and I'm tryin' to figure
Why the talk about breedin', brands, and hybrid vigor?

93

She tells me about anecdotes and just what's needed
To have bad contractions and malapropisms deleted.
I said, Ma'am, if somethin's that sick, why you can bet,
I'll be gettin' the antidote needed—from a vet.

So, then she gets real personal, and starts onto me.
Said I had a danglin' participle that was plain to see.
Well, I got so red faced. Damn, I couldn't even reply.
Then I looked all around and—even checked my fly.

And that's when I had enough of this English course.
Why, it would make more sense a talkin' to my horse.
So, we rode outa there with our participles danglin'.
Hell, I don't want to be a poet. I'm just word wranglin'!

NEVER EAT ORANGES!

Did you ever notice when a ride gets long
or a hunt begins to drag,
how your guide will pull an apple or orange
from his own saddle bag?

He'll unfold his Buck, then carve 'er up
in four quarters neat and nice,
with hand outstretched, eyeball the dudes,
and insist they take a slice.

The greenhorns to this adventurous gang act
with zest to his tempting morsel,
slam 'er down the hatch with a toast to health
on its way to their twisting torso.

But, the old hands keep their distance like
an old mule you might try to halter.
Regardless sweet juicy tempts and chides,
in negative response they never falter.

"No," they say, "I've got my own," or the Doc
says it gives 'em a sporadic liver.
It's not that they don't partake of fruit.
It's the guide's knife that makes 'em quiver.

Just watch this salty mountain gent as he
goes about his backcountry duties,
And heed the ways he wields that knife.
You'll find he has some beauties!

He'll pick up a horse's gimpy foot, and
commence to clean out all the crud.
Your nose says bet that scraped out
stuff (sniff) surely ain't all mud.

He'll take your daily catch of trout,
slit and clean them in one sitting.
Then cut through the shiny pile that's
left, just to see what the fish were hitting.

He'll set a screw in your fishing reel,
cut the twine from alfalfa bales,
splice reins, scrape the bot eggs from horses'
hair, and clean his fingernails.

He'll cut bandages from an old wound, and
use the blade to bell a mule,
skin an elk, pry the caps off fly repellent
and the cans of Coleman fuel.

"Don't you think you should wash your knife?"
You offer him this warning.
"Sure," he nods, "I boiled it in the coffee pot,
just the other morning."

He looks at you, then smiles and winks, says,
"Just kiddin', I don't really mean it.
When I think my ol' Buck needs a change of
oil, I slice an orange to clean it."

So if your guide offers an apple slice,
just smile and say, "Of course."
Then ease off gently away from the group,
and feed it to your horse.

But, if an orange slice is his only gift, and
now your gut's not feelin' placid,
it's time to develop a sudden allergy
to all forms of citric acid.

IF A FISH FELL IN A FOREST

(If a tree falls in a forest, and no one is there to hear it, does it
make a sound?)

"Are you bound for Boulder?" the lady asked
as she stepped to the trail's side.
"No Ma'am," I smiled, "to the basin beyond,
a couple more hours' ride."

She glared through me to the fishing rods
lashed to the packs of the ol' mule string.
Said, "How's the fishing been in the distant lake?
You been catching anything?"

"Not good," I lied, as I winked to the guests
in true angling tradition.
"Why Jacques Cousteau couldn't find a trout there
on a high powered expedition."

"The fishing there was wonderful," she snapped,
"before the likes of you came along.
You see no one ever visited that lake,
and the trout were big and strong."

Well, I bit my tongue, and laughed to myself
and held back my rebuttal.
I thought, "Lady, why don't you just say what you think
and not be so doggone subtle."

I wondered how many fingerlings she'd packed in there,
or how many limits they packed out?
Had she ever donated for elk and sheep habit,
to D.U. or the Trout?

But rudeness in the backcountry is just
another form of air pollution.
And, to pollute her day in return,
would not be a proud solution.

So, I visited a couple minutes more and said,
"Ma'am, please have a nice day.
I hope that you enjoy your hike."
And then we went along our way.

But, as I rode away, her words came back
and started my weak mind to thinkin'.
I wondered, did I really hear her right?
I know I ain't been drinkin'.

A fine fishing hole where no one'd go
seemed like a great riddle to me.
Like, is there a sound made, if no one is there
to hear the fallin' of a tree?

In this mythical scene, pristine, serene,
hungry trout would feed all day.
Cutthroats, brookies, 'bows, and browns
would race to devour their prey.

These aquatic hogs with girths like logs
might eat beaver, frog, or duck.
Their excessive might and aggressive appetite
would assure an angler fun and luck.

And, if this sportsman's heaven existed to fulfill
all an angler's dreams and wishing,
but no one ever wet a line there,
could it still be called "great fishing"?

And, if you were the emperor of this land,
a king or queen, or the maharishi,
the big chief, the Pope, the C.E.O.,
the high priest of all that's fishy,

And you found this pristine water body
of angling quality as we'd all wish it,
would it be fair, would it be right,
if only you were allowed to fish it?

Now, I'm happy to be from a land that's free,
and share a forest that is ours.
But, the day you'd take my privilege away,
you're on the way to losing yours!

For Whom the Bells Toll...and Toll...and Toll

It must have been 1988
on a cold November morning.
At our hunting camp up on Fossil Ridge,
we were awakened without warning.
"Time to rise and shine, boys! It's 3:00 a.m.
The elk are gettin' away.
You're burning daylight." He kicked our cots.
"We've used up half the day."
I came to, like I'd been shot at, and screamed,
"What the hell's goin' on?"
Did the horses run off? Is there a bear in the camp?
Somethin' must be wrong.
The flashlight's glare made our faces stare
like deer in the headlight's beam,
with one arm outstretched and squinty frowns
as if thrust from a nightmare dream.
There stood this big man. His name was Ray.
He had a grin from ear to ear.
With teeth clenched like a pack of wolves,
we growled, "Ray, get outa here!
We've still got half an hour more to sleep.
It's three hours before daylight."
But, Ray persisted with his perverse joke
until the boys got on the fight.
There were 10 new cuss words invented
on the spot, that I'd never heard before.
A piece of firewood hit the stiff tent flap
as Ray ducked outside the door.
Our sleepin' was done so we jumped up.

It took snarls and few minutes to dress us.
After three long hard seasons from dark to dark,
each second of sleep was precious.
Now, we ain't strangers to practical jokes,
but this one tourist had best be believin',
If you want to play games just remember,
some cowboys don't play just for even.
Let me take him to East Beaver, Clay offered,
through the blow down, bogs and tumble.
When he crawls his backside out of there tonight,
he'll be a sight more humble.
"Let's saddle him up on Ol' Widowmaker," Al said,
"That'll be a fun sight to see."
"He'll starve to death 'fore he comes back down,"
we all laughed with glee.
"Why not leave the cinch loose on that barrel
shaped mare. Hell, Ray'll never know.
By the time we've ridden a couple of miles,
we'll have had us a real rodeo."
"Boys," I said, "those are some temptin' ideas.
But with danger we don't dare flirt.
Oh, we're gonna make Ray feel some pain,
but let's don't let no one get hurt.
Let's saddle these horses and get ready to hunt.
We'll think on this all day.
We'll catch him when he's least expectin' it.
Yes, ol' Ray has got to pay!"
The hunters drifted back to camp near dark.
We'd all put in a tough cold day.
We went right to work on our wranglin' chores.
No one's mind was on horseplay.
I suggested that we keep the night horses tied.

They could use some extra feed.
We'll come turn 'em out right after chuck,
and throw 'em the pellets they need.
Dinner was great. The cook tent was fun
with the usual stories, jokes and laughter.
But the dudes were tired and left for their tents
to turn in shortly thereafter.
And, that's when we put our plan into action.
We all met at the horse corral.
Two of us grabbed bags of alfalfa pellets.
The rest fit each horse with a bell.
We scattered those hay cubes in neat little piles
all around Ray's sleepin' tent.
Then turned loose that herd of cowbell clad clangers;
and after the pellets they went.
The horses charged that tent with a vengeance.
We chuckled when we heard a squall,
hoofbeats, yells, and bells aringin', like
the Salvation Army attackin' a mall.
All night long the ponies pawed for those pellets.
The boys and I really slept well.
It's relaxin' to know that your mounts are nearby,
by the tolling from a night bell.
Ray's tentmates weren't what you'd call cheerful
over the fix that he got them in.
Oh, they'd cawed when hearin' of Ray's joke on us,
but now they'd no cause to grin.
Sayin', "Ray, you ought to hung from the
                gamepole outside.
Here's a promise we will keep.
You'll be gunshot and quartered if ever again
you mess with the wranglers' sleep."

Next morning at breakfast the smilin' guides asked,
"Hey Ray, did ya sleep okay?"
But the long-faced joker ignored their smug probes.
He had not a word to say.
"Men," I said, "Ray can't hear your query
and much less your laughter and your singin'.
Why, Doc says it's a sure sign of goin' deaf when
your ears hear a constant ringin'."

TEED OFF

Lonnie up and moved away.
He said he couldn't stand
the encroachment of these newcomers
and their attitude toward land.

He was foaled here in the Rockies.
Cut his teeth on horses' hide.
He loved horses, loved his cattle,
loved to ranch and rope and ride.

He re-rooted in Oklahoma.
To the flatlands he chose to roam.
I'd bet Hell froze over the very day
he left his mountain home.

Well today it finally dawned on me
how he knew to change his song.
With snow gone from the horse pasture,
there were signs of somethin' wrong.

And that sign had popped up everywhere.
Hundreds of 'em, and ain't that funny.
I'd swear that we had been attacked
by a prolific Easter Bunny.

Or was it something the horses ate
and passed through them in time,
to dye those roadapples with red stripes,
pure white, blaze orange, and lime.

I gathered in some samples,
for close inspection and to scrutinize.
And, now the reason for Lonnie's retreat
is not such a great surprise.

So listen up, my ranchin' friends,
and heed the signs of impending disaster.
The time has come to quit the country when
you're findin' golf balls in your pasture.

If You Knew September

I wish you knew September
from a trail up near the sky,
and knew that thrill and tingle
of a Rocky Mountain high.

Oh, you should know September's slopes
blessed by aspen trees,
and partake the mountain's medicine
as heart and mind it frees.

I wish you knew the power
of this hardened dapple grey
strengthened by the golden glow
of a cool crisp Autumn day.

Oh, you should know September's sun
as it bathes your cares away
astride a sturdy mountain horse
with gentle rocking sway.

I wish you knew the coyote's verse
of the old time siren song,
and knew the pack's camaraderie,
felt the urge to sing along.

Oh, you should know the passion
of the bull elk's shrill reply
that tugs at vestiges of your ancient soul
lost to time gone by.

How I wish you knew September
from times spent near the wild,
and knew a life close to a place
where God and nature smiled.

For if you knew September
in the way it's meant to be,
You'd leave convention far behind
to be riding here with me.

DAVID J. ROTHMAN

David J. Rothman was born in Northampton, Massachusetts in 1959. He earned an A.B. cum laude in History and Literature at Harvard University in 1982, an M.A. in English at the University of Utah in 1984, and a Ph.D. in English at New York University in 1992. He has taught courses in literature and writing at the University of Utah, Zhejiang University (People's Republic of China), New York University, Western State College of Colorado, and several secondary schools. His poems and essays have appeared widely. He is co-founder, with Charles Stegeman, of the Western Slope Summer Music Festival.

He is currently Headmaster of Crested Butte Academy and Executive Director of the Robinson Jeffers Association. He lives in Crested Butte, Colorado with his wife Emily and son Jacob.

YOUTH

I'm wiser now. So what? It's like the rack.
I loved my stupid youth, its limber luck.
I want my perfect love and anger back.

Each day was like a bone that I could crack,
Each night a ripe fruit I could bite and suck.
I'm wiser now. So what? It's like the rack.

Give me green dreams, blue dreams, in my dark shack.
Give me another chance to run amok.
I want my perfect love and anger back.

It's true the world gives in, breaks down, goes black,
And I acknowledge what the years will pluck:
I'm wiser now. So what? It's like the rack,

To know the end of life's a zippered sack,
To know that even love slows and gets stuck.
I want my perfect love and anger back:

I'd be again a blossoming lilac,
Lunatic, lover, poet, friend of Puck.
I'm wiser now. So what? It's like the rack.
I want my perfect love and anger back.

LET IT SNOW

Let it snow. Let blue skies fade to steel.
Let the wind gust, then pick up, flat light creep in.
Let clouds arrive, pile up, grow dark, conceal.
Let the weather service issue a bulletin.
Let the first flakes fall like the kiss in a seduction,
Full of promise, tenderness, and danger.
Let them whisper imminent destruction,
Then unfurl their fiery love and anger.
Let evening fall, let freedom ring, let things
Break down berserk, dark spirals bust out big,
And flake on flailing flake sculpt thickening rings
Of snow beyond what any plow can dig.
The ground is bare, the flowers dead. Let's go:
It's winter, time for blizzards. Let it snow.

WHISTLING IN JANUARY

The ice inside the window seems forever.
   Transmission fluid slows to tired glue.
   At dusk the sky gives up its weak, thin blue.
   The stars shine off the mercury at never.
The earth obeys its dark, tremendous lever.
   The skating on the lake is fast and true.
   Dogs whine, limp, bite their paws, and call to you.
   Things stiffen, harden, halt, stop, break, and sever.
But larger than its hour, and more than ice,
   Beyond its temporary shape and end,
   Only itself, away from which it's slipping,
Time passing and arriving at a price
   That's still a moving sign of how we'd bend:
   One icicle in the new sun, slowly dripping.

WHEN THE WIND AND DARK WAVES COME

1.

Be gentle when the wind and dark waves come.
Be gentle in the inhuman house of stone.
Be gentle though you will still be alone.
Be gentle even if it strikes you dumb.

Let that arc be your dream among the trees.
Let it be the underlying song.
Let it be a fiction, but not wrong.
Let it be the lie which cannot freeze.

Your time grows shorter as you read these letters.
The sun is throwing shadows down the floor.
Even oceans crack beneath time's thumb.
Yet here's a choice, within relentless fetters:
Deny each other and the bad world, or
Be gentle when the wind and dark waves come.

2.

Be angry when the wind and dark waves come.
Be angry in the inhuman house of stone.
Be angry though you will still be alone.
Be angry even if it strikes you dumb.

Let that arc be your dream among the trees.
Let it be the underlying song.
Let it be a fiction, but not wrong.
Let it be the lie which cannot freeze.

Your time grows shorter as you read these letters.
The sun is throwing shadows down the floor.
Even oceans crack beneath time's thumb.
Yet here's a choice, within relentless fetters:
Lie down quietly forever, or
Be angry when the wind and dark waves come.

Resurrection of a Mouse

What full, sad sounds, the noise that you were making,
Clenched in our cat's jaws, pierced by a tooth,
Inevitably caught forever, shaking
And squeaking like a man who's seen the truth.
Sneaky pest who shit all over tables,
Vermin, host to rabies, hanta, louse,
I'm undeceived by all the mousy fables.
I'm glad you're gone, I'm pleased our cat can mouse.
Still, I cannot forget your empty death,
Prey to the satisfied play of calico.
Years later I start awake, hearing your breath
Cry life as far as any voice can go.
    Confidently soaring, writing with my wing,
    Beyond all praise and blame, you sing, you sing.

ONE OF THE LORDS OF LIFE

Peace to all living things,
I scribbled in the log on Vulture Peak
Because time was short and it was true.
Then I stood, like any American, alone,
To be in that immense desert glow.
Down into dusk, the Hieroglyphics and the White Tanks,
The Big Horns, the Harquehalas, and the Bradshaws
Offered bent, brown rock, forests of saguaros,
And hidden life to the emerging stars.

Lampless, I turned and scrambled three-point
Down the chimney, blaze to blaze,
Until I met the saddle dirt,
Then bounded down a crooked trail
Into the darkness growing visible.

A whisper in the shape of a green branch
Lay before me. Wonder not, it said.
And so I did not wait, although it ruled the path.
I had no chance to stop and listen
To the quiet voices of my education.
Only when I landed on my right foot
One runner's pace above did it become
A sinuous emperor of emerald
Warming himself on a rock in the patience
Of silence, cunning, and exile.

Nature does not suffer decay: always new,
Unlike the memory on which minds turn,
It unfolds like emptiness.
One word, his name, sparked from nowhere

And sank into my foot.
A hand reached down, carved wings,
Then plucked my muscles with more light.
Too big for dinner, too sudden for his surprise
To coil up and rattle out an argument,
I jumped into the current of our doing.
Pebbles tinkled like dice
As I leapt over the fat green snake
Who squirmed silently beneath my soles
Like a piece of animal cactus,
And I did not fall, I landed with a gravel crunch
Between the cacti, unstung, miraculously erect,
No mouth of numbing ash, no broken ankle,
Below the double distance a rattler can strike.

Strange alteration in me. The fruit was praise.
Mojave green: I do not think I missed my chance
With you, but took it where it lay—
As if I had the choice.
You are still prompting my words
Away from deep, high speculation
And into one breath after another—
The coincidence of dusk and sage,
The distant glow of Phoenix, and the dying sun.
As I climb slowly up into these thoughts,
Remembering my long, headlong descent,
On which I lost the trail, then found it again
And walked out from the mountains in darkness,
I see you turning, raising your head in cold curiosity
As I vanish beneath your jaw, and I hear you calling
          my name,
Although you are ignorant of it.

THE SHAPE OF WATER MOST LIKE LOVE

Rain is not the shape of water most like love,
For rain nourishes fields
Or destroys them with indifferent passion.
The sky wears rain on its sleeve.
Powerful and beautiful, but capricious,
Requiring rainbows to reassure us,
Rain is not love—
Only a love affair.

The ocean is not the shape of water most like love,
For it is love's destination.
Although the realm of birth, each ocean touches
Every shore and action, named or not.
A form of everything,
Yet unable to create more of itself,
The ocean is not love—
Love is but one part of its history.

Ice is not the shape of water most like love,
For ice is like what is called thinking,
A patient architecture made from what already exists.
Mostly at opposite poles, or high on rock,
Ice is not love—it broods too far away
To discover anything greater than itself.

Lakes are too inward, rivers divide.
Crystals of snow all break and decay.
Clouds and fog by definition drift.

What is the shape of water most like love?
Hurricanes, unfathered depths, and polar caps
Only churn what has another source,
The drops formed one by one for the first time,
In infinite darkness and under irresistible force.

And you, who are mostly water,
In your unrelenting solitude coupled with movement,
Although you might do anything,
Still resemble a spring
More than you resemble rain, or the ocean,
Or an immense, distant river of ice.

JAMES TIPTON

James Tipton lives on a high mesa in western Colorado where he keeps bees and writes poems. His work is widely published, including credits in *The Nation*, *South Dakota Review*, *Southern Humanities Review*, *The Greensboro Review*, *Esquire*, *Field*, and *American Literary Review*; and also in various anthologies and other works, most recently *Aphrodite*, by Isabel Allende (1998), and *Bleeding Hearts*, edited by Michelle Lovric (1998). He wrote a chapbook titled *The Wizard of Is* (Bread & Butter Press, 1995). His most recent collection of poems, *Letters from a Stranger* (Conundrum Press, 1998), won the 1999 Colorado Book Award for Poetry. He is currently working on *No Thoroughfare Canyon*.

I Want to Speak with the Blood that Lies Down

> Yo quiero hablar con muchas cosas
> y no me iré de este planeta
> sin saber qué vine a buscar...
>
> *I want to speak with many things*
> *and I will not leave this planet*
> *without knowing what I came to find...*
>
> Pablo Neruda, "Bestiario"

I want to speak with the blood that lies down
each night to sleep inside your heart; I want to speak
with these words that procreate like rabbits
when I think of you; I want to speak with your
      virginal ribs,
with the hand inside; I want to devour the mud
      that mocks
all diamond flesh; I want to find a prayer that sticks,
a clock that ticks only love, a time
that turns this desperation into peace, a book
with the moon on every page that only we
can read together; I want to speak in one
interminable sentence that can be understood
in a single sitting; I want to speak with
the tired angels that live inside the shoulders
of tiny children; I want to speak with cripples
that meet in laundromats late at night looking
for little boxes of soap; I want to speak with
these clothes before I join them; I want to find
the delicate violet that rises out of the dead volcano;

I want to find the verb that shakes me loose,
the noun that is the place I live, the
comma that joins me with you; I want
to speak softly and thoroughly, and be clearly
in you; I want to speak with apples and honey
and silver and snow—I want every thing to stop
for a moment destined for you and for me,
for a time when we, butchered at birth,
come back to life, rescued at last
like children in a miraculous fairy tale—
I want to speak with the dead, who move
like leaves in this night that blows its rapture
toward the dislocated sea; I want to speak
with the forgotten spring, with the light
in the dead comet; I want to speak with salt
and with the teeth I found in the desert and with
wounded silence, ravenous solitude;
I want to speak with Pablo Neruda and Christ,
and with the idiot brother of God, and with the tunnel
at the foot of the bed, with the corridors
of all longing; I want to speak with these long nights
of useless letters, with these boots that walk without me
when I rest, and with the spirits that shake these feet
when I lay me down to weep; I want to speak with the
thirsty rain, the lonely garbage, the tire that remembers
when it was a tree in Brazil; I want to speak with
the fragrance of sage that rises up, late into the night,
after a soft rain; I want to speak with cinnamon
and chocolate, and with windows that do not open,
and with the bag of hair in the shop of the old barber;

I want to speak with the dance that rises
in this body when, like a distant bell
come home, your letter rings in me whatever
matters; I want to whisper "love…love…love"
while this very hand is stretched to Sausalito,
cradling your heart in sleep.

THERE ARE RIVERS OF ORANGES

There are rivers of oranges, sweet
like the autumn sun, sweet
like the sand on the doubloon
found at the bottom of sleep,
like the sweet stars we delicately peel,
like the roots of acorn squash,
like the eyes of the jaguars in Peru.

Maybe when we deeply imagine
we no longer imagine at all,
but dive, at last, naked and alive,
into the flesh of oranges, into
the steaming jungle, into words
that hang like orange rain,
like love just before it happens.

It is everything we ever wanted
to remember, like empty orange
file folders, labeled "Careers," like
the lover who walks backwards
through every shift of love until
he arrives home, to the place
where what is seen inside is what is.

There the orange mind bursts
like a village of chrysanthemums
gone mad, or gathered together
for mass, praising the
orange hands of God, praising
the saffron eyes of the flower saints,
praising the hearts in the tiny seeds.

I Wanted You in the Kitchen of My Heart

I wanted you in the kitchen of my heart;
and there, after many cold lunches,
I found you; and there, like herbs
undressing in soup, I came to love you;
and there, like a delicate tea
of mangoes and marigolds your mouth
opened, and your words, flecked with gold
and the eroticism of your Latin blood,
flowed, like the blood I longed for, into me.

And how could I lose you among these cups
and spoons, among these golden candles,
these jars of honey lined along the window?
And what forget-me-nots in winter
tie me to you still? I could die in this bread
I have made without you. For you I would burn
this dry brain for incense; I would
serve you the wine inside the night; I would
drink the sea to give you salt.

Te Quería en la Cocina de mi Corazón

Te quería en la cocina de mi corazón;
y allí, después de muchos almuerzos fríos,
te encontré; y allí, como hierbas
desnudándose en la sopa, llegué a amarte;
y allí, como un delicado té
de mangos y caléndulas, tu boca
se abrió y tus palabras, salpicadas de oro
y del erotisimo de tu sangre latina,
se derramaron, como las sangre que añoraba, en mí.

¿Y cómo podría perderte entre estas tazas
y cucharas, entere estas velas doradas,
estos frascos de miel alineados en la ventana?
¿Y qué nomeolvides en invierno
me atan aún a ti? Podría morir en este pan
que he hecho sin ti. Por ti quemaría
como incienso este cerebro seco; te serviría
el vino de la noche; bebería
el mar para darte sal.

(traducido por Isabel Allende)

MARK TODD

Writers' Web West says Mark Todd's poetry "is some of the most evocative, well-paced writing among the genre [of poetry about the West]," and acclaimed southwestern poet Keith Wilson called Todd's verse "worthy of Gary Snyder at his best…"

Mark Todd is a twelve–year resident of Colorado's Western Slope and lives in a ranching community just below the Continental Divide and thirty miles from Gunnison, where he is a professor of English at Western State College and serves as chair of the Department of Communication Arts, Languages, and Literature.

WIRE SONG

The country here-abouts
Can be told best in wire.

It's a history that's spun
In ways books seldom bind,
In ways where the knowing
Of this land's recounted
In strands with barbs for bards.

Wire stories our telling
By twisting those legends
Of posts smacked split-rock hard,
Pounded and then sturdied,
Wedged with flint and talus.

Wire can plot straights of line
Through boundaried stretches
Over ground that's broken
With ditch and arroyo.

It smoothes the sense of harsh
And unforgiving land,
The stumble through pastured
Grasses fed by stone-fast
Roots, by tangles of brush.

Taut and strong in the wind,
Wire strings tales from steel yarn,
Singing the lines of place
Through rusted, untold words.

THE GAME TRAIL

There! She says and
Sure enough, up the gouge
Of Barret Creek, the soft
Honk-like calls of cow elk
To calves, their great tan
And white bulk speckled
With the shadowcast of aspen.
We work uphill, upwind
Over sage and talus,
Over a trail made by game,
My stepdaughter scrambling
Ahead, me trying to close ranks,
To share a common space.
I stumble often in this uneasy
Journey, one that reaches
Past today's late afternoon sun.
I know the tug of thread
Between us often snaps,
And I lose the way connecting,
Our paths, we both standing
Distantly, side by side.
But there are moments
Like today, when we surprise
Ourselves surprising elk,
Face to face in a stumbled-on
Clearing of common ground.

SON ET LUMIÈRE

It's in the featureless
Lay of the great High Plains
That heads of anvilled storm
Vault full afternoon blown,
That the flat face of land
Brushes sky into gust-
Borne scenery, that new-
Born free-form horizons
Can merge a somehow ground
With the fastened texture
Of a darkening thunder,
With those lightning-stroke sparks,
Through glimpsed-fire discharges,
A living-almost thing,
A filled-wonder billow
Heavy with the weightless,
Touchless belch of a breath
That closes southwest days.

MUD SEASON

Tires chew into the soft,
April earth, drop easily
into ruts that sluice
the passages of spring
through country roads.

The fields still linger
with five months' snowwash,
stock trails crisscrossing
the meadow-white. No longer
content with aging bales,

the horses search, paw
at the crust thaw, hungering
for the shootgreen grass
that surely lies beneath.
Across the pasture

I ease the truck
toward their gate,
a weary struggle
against mud channels
that later will lead to home.

To Kill Stray Dogs

Stomping to the house
a mile-away neighbor
lets the mad of his .30-06
point straight at our dogs.

Seems he's found five
calves, bone-licked clean,
their lipless baby teeth
grimacing at the dull sky
of winter. Not enough
leftover flesh and hide
for coyote work, he says,
knowing full well it's
our dogs live closest by.

But we've seen the pack
whose hunger could run down
the fall size of spring heifers.
Not two days before, three
dogs chased our daughter's pick-up,
as if a pick-up could rescue
the lost from their eyes.

But now their tongues
too much taste the salt
of fresh kill—they'll get
no stockgrower's pity. Now,
I, too, must harden
the dog-soft of my heart
(or I may wake one night
to snarls that tear at the legs
of our weanling filly), must go
with the party that will hunt
them from this valley...

Tonight my head shifts,
turns upon a comfortless bed.
My dreams search the hills
and drainages to the east
of our place, restless until
they see the three dark forms:
forms that lie still, silent
under the huddle and gray
of a splash-cold moon.

RIGBY

It was the time that Rigby
(Sixteen hands so bay and shiny)
First saw cattle.
Seven years old but still box-stall baby.
Ears quivering to hooves,
Caprioling over bunch grass,
Not knowing that heifers,
All doe-eyed and curious,
Would not thunder their numbers
Through barbed wire and get him.

Rigby
       bringing to pasture a schooling
       of groomed earth of race track,
And me
       his gentrified, unschooled equal—

How comical we must have seemed
To ranch neighbors, polite but smiling,
As they watched us both that summer day
While we tried to walk a country road.

GRANDMOTHER'S FARM

The door jamb still frames
The scorch of concrete,
Of fixed timber—
What is left
Of my grandmother's house.

A propane leak, they said.
Too far from town
For fire fighters, too old
And weathered to save.

My cousin and uncle
Later torched the rest,
The blaze driving out
Scores of rats
From corn crib and barn.
Their soot-smeared bodies
Charcoaled the winter ground
With lines of retreat:
Target practice
Under a frozen,
Panhandle sky.

A day when snow mingled
With ash and blood.

POST SCRIPTUM

for my father

There are always
            questions
One would ask when lips
Are silent
            bones cold
In the earth.

Scud clouds shuffle by:
Harbingers of winds that
Will scrape the ground tonight,
Tugging at soft sod,
At memories that refuse
            to lie
As quietly.

ROSEMERRY WAHTOLA TROMMER

Even though she'd always wanted to be a poet, Rosemerry Wahtola Trommer went to The Colorado College to become a doctor. She came out with an English degree and went on to earn a Master's degree in English Language and Linguistics at the University of Wisconsin-Madison before deciding to take the risk and start writing for a living.

In 1994, she moved to Telluride, Colorado. She's worked as a journalist, newspaper editor and magazine editor. She now writes freelance articles for magazines, edits books and writes a weekly column on the English language for the local newspaper. Since 1998, she's served as the director for the Telluride Writers' Guild.

Through all years, writing and performing poetry has remained a pleasure. Rosemerry leads a poetry discussion series at the local library, teaches poetry classes for children and adults, has published her works in numerous journals and has two books of poetry. Her first book, *lunaria* (Sisu Press, 1999), is in its second printing. The second, *if you listen: poetry & photographs of the san juan mountains* (Western Reflections Press, 2000), features an introduction by ecological jazz musician Paul Winter and black-and-white photographs by Eileen Benjamin.

SONNET FOR JULY

today I'm your queen
you crown me with nettles
thistles ring my neck
in purple mockery

it's a prickery love
in our kingdom today
we've let weeds thrive
around our thrones

but king of my blood
we live in this castle together
and know this:
I love you best naked
and know this:
my rose garden blooms

IF YOU LISTEN

the snow falls with
no sound

standing outside
in its silence
you find yourself
listening
to listening

but oh,
the snow knows symphony
its score is written on
every mountain, every tree
each rooftop, each street
as each snowflake falls
a silent beat
a voiceless song
composed by sky
performed by icicle,
avalanche,
slush and ski

if you listen
you'll hear it echoing
the snow is silent
and still
it sings

MARCH

in winter evenings
we dream of rivers
of waters that wind us
slowly toward we

wanting the water
the wanton swirls waiting
we whisper the names
of the wheres we will go

westwater, salmon
cataract canyon
san juan, dolores

we chant them like spells
until summer swells
warm waves in march blood

CLIMBING THE RIDGE

"write what you know"—an ode to Lax

one step
one step
i stop
i take
one breath
one breath
warm sun
above
white snow
below
i breathe
i take
one step
one step